from a kid's experience

Papua New Guinea

The land of the unexpected

Núria Cort Lluís

DEDICATION

To our twin daughters, Clàudia and Júlia, who constantly amaze us, source of laughter and primary inspiration of love. Joy to the whole family.

CONTENTS

Introduction

My cheeky and adventurous twin sister, Clàudia, is from Spain.

We were born on the same day, in the same place.

I arrived just after Clàudia.

Wah Wah Wah... the loudest kid ever... that's me, Júlia.

For this ridiculous amount of time difference, I will have to accept all my life that she is the eldest... but... it's ok because I am the biggest.

People like to guess who is the eldest and only some get it right.

Others like to play with us and guess who is who?

As if we were identical!

We are not identical guys! We are... fra-ter-nal.

We are very different.

Can't you see I don't have a fringe?

When people ask me that dreaded question again...

Júlia, where are you from?

I need to clarify...

Do you mean where was I born?

Or where have I grown up?

Or how many passports do I hold?

Because although we were born in Catalonia, Spain, we have lived in several countries.

We are often called "Third culture kids" because we have Spanish culture from our mum, Australian culture from our dad and we live in a third country. Have you heard about this term before?

Maybe you are one of these kids?

Anyway... currently I live in Port Moresby, the capital of Papua New Guinea, which is a very long name for a country.

That´s why it's often called PNG.

Very few countries have three words in their name.

Do you know any other country with three words in its name?

I like geography and there are only three more in the whole world!

Here, we have friends from PNG and from all over the world because they came with their parents who work and live in this beautiful country.

We are called ex-pats (short for expatriate) which means we are living temporarily in a country that is not our own country.

Through our friends we learnt interesting facts about their way of living in PNG, in Australia, India, Fiji, Philippines, France, England, New Zealand, South Africa, USA, Latin American countries and many more.

How great!

We all have different traditions, and it is fun playing together.

We celebrate diversity and differences.

Sometimes we like dancing with a dot
on our forehead pretending to be
Niranjana, our friend from India...

Sometimes we pretend to
make Lamingtons in our little
kitchen, the delicious
Australian cake.

Sometimes we put little Andy in a bilum
and pretend to be his mummy.

Little Andy is the son of our beloved auntie, Lisa, our nanny, or Haus Meri as it is called in PNG.

She is part of our family.

We all want to be little Andy's mum at the same time... but that's ok because this is how it is here in PNG anyway.

Kids can call more than one person "mum".

Do you know what a bilum is?

Do you know why kids can call "mum" to more than one person here?

Do you know how kids are named?

Would you like to know more about PNG, commonly known as The Land of the Unexpected?

Are you ready?

Guess what?

You only need to turn the page.

GREENLAND
UNITED STATES
CANADA
UNITED STATES
MEXICO
ICELAND
IRELAND
D
U.K
FR
PORTUGAL
SPAIN
MOROCCO
A
WESTERN SAHARA
MAURITANIA
MALI
SENEGAL
G
VENEZUELA
GUYANA
SURINAME
FRENCH GULANA
COLOMBIA
ECUADOR
PERU
BRAZIL
BOLIVIA
PARAGUAY
CHILE
URUGUAY
ARGENTINA

FINLAND
EDEN
OLAND
UKRAINE
OMANIA
RUSSIA
KAZAKHSTAN
MONGOLIA
TURKEY
GREECE
CYPRUS
LEBANON
IRAN
IRAQ
KUWAIT
QATAR
PAKISTAN
NEPAL
CHINA
KOREA
JAPAN
EGYPT
SAUDI
ARABIA
U.A.E
INDIA
VIETNAM
LAOS
TAIWAN
SUDAN
YEMEN
THAILAND
CAMBODIA
PHILIPPINES
A.R
EQUATORIAL
ETHIOPIA
KENYA
SRI
LANKA
MALAYASIA
ONGO
OLA
ZAMBIA
MALAWI
MADAGASCAR
INDONESIA
PAPUA
NEW GUINEA
SOLOMON
ISLANDS
BOTSWANA
MOZAMBIQUE
SOUTH
AFRICA
FIJI
AUSTRALIA
NEW
ZEALAND
INDONESIA
Port
Moresby

1. Where is Papua New Guinea?

PNG is a country in Oceania, located north of Australia. Since Australia is considered a continent rather than an island, the largest island in Oceania is called New Guinea.

Papua New Guinea occupies the eastern half of this island, called the mainland, where most of PNG's population lives.

The western half of New Guinea island is part of Indonesia, which is another country.

PNG is made up of its mainland and over 600 islands, both large and small.

Port Moresby, the capital city, also known as POM, is in PNG mainland.

In Papua New Guinea there are 22 provinces, which are divided into 4 regions:

1. Highlands Region: Simbu, Eastern Highlands, Enga, Hela, Jiwaka, Southern Highlands and Western Highlands.

2. Islands Region: East New Britain, Manus, New Ireland, Bougainville and West New Britain.

3. Momase Region: Morobe, Madang, East Sepik and West Sepik. (Notice how each province uses two letters from the region's name to form its own)

4. Southern Region: Central, Gulf, Milne Bay, Northern Province (Oro), Western (Fly) and the National Capital District or Port Moresby.

My sister Clàudia and I had to check our large, laminated world map stuck on the wall next to our bathtub, to locate PNG.

While playing in the bath, we discovered that Papua New Guinea is remarkably close to Australia, with the Torres Strait Islands—an Australian archipelago — positioned between them.

Dad says that the shortest stretch between these islands and PNG is about 4 kilometres, like doing 10 laps in a standard running track.

Mummy likes to compare distances in pool laps, so she says that 4 km is the distance of swimming 80 laps in a 50-meter pool.

I can imagine a skilled, brave and adventurous swimmer traversing this gap in about an hour, but while possible, it would be incredibly risky and dangerous.

Can you guess why? Because while crossing open water you can find unpredictable currents, sudden storms, powerful winds, sharks, crocodiles, and jellyfish… so… it might not be the best idea ever! So… we decided to get there by plane instead.

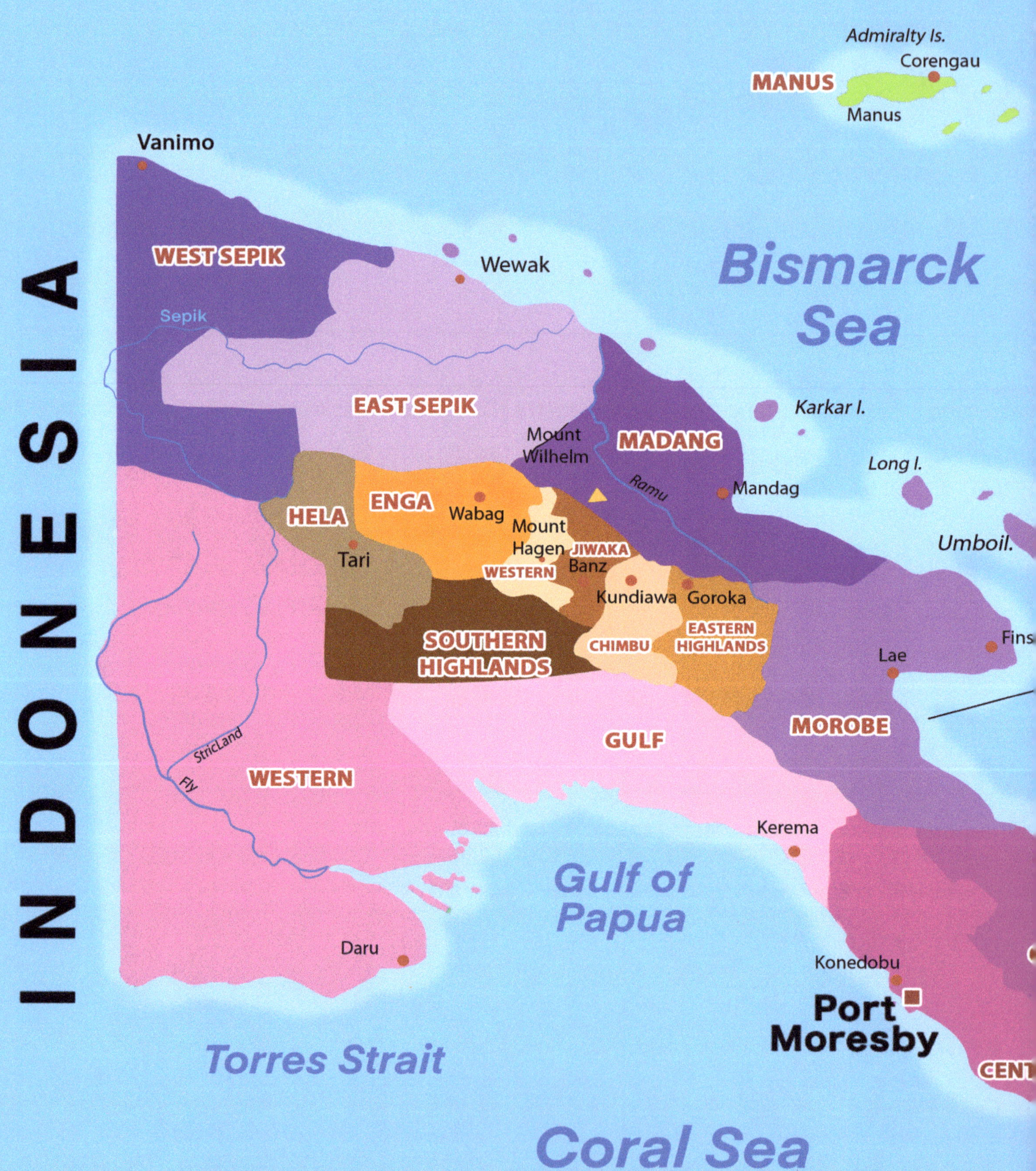

Admiralty Is.
Corengau
MANUS
Manus
Vanimo
Bismarck Sea
WEST SEPIK
Wewak
Sepik
Karkar I.
EAST SEPIK
MADANG
Long I.
Mount Wilhelm
Ramu
Mandag
HELA
ENGA
Wabag
Mount Hagen
JIWAKA
Banz
Umboil.
Tari
WESTERN
Kundiawa
Goroka
CHIMBU
EASTERN HIGHLANDS
SOUTHERN HIGHLANDS
Fins
Lae
StricLand
GULF
MOROBE
Fly
WESTERN
Kerema
Gulf of Papua
Daru
Konedobu
Port Moresby
Torres Strait
CENT
Coral Sea
INDONESIA

St Matthias Group
New Hanover
Kavieng
NEW IRELAND
Namatanai
Rabaul Kokopo
WEST NEW BRITAIN
Kimbe
NEW BRITAIN
EAST NEW BRITAIN
Kandrian
uman Gulf
Buka Island
Bougainville Island
BOUGAINVILLE
Kieta
Solomon Sea
PAPUA NEW GUINEA
detta
Trobriand Is.
Goodenough I.
D'Entrecasteaux Is.
Fergusson I.
Normanby I.
Alotau
MILNE BAY
Louisiade Archipelago
Misima I.
Togula I.
Rossel I.
Islands
Momase
Southern
Highlands

2. How do you get to PNG and travel around?

You can get to PNG by plane or by boat.

In PNG there are tall mountains, volcanos, lakes and big rivers.

Most of the country is covered by tropical rainforest with no roads to go from one town to another.

Many of the remote villages do not have roads or an airstrip. Local people walk for days or travel on the waterways by canoe or small boats, to get to larger villages or towns for food supplies or medical attention.

More than 80% of Papua New Guinian people live in the rural areas.

When we arrived in the capital, warm, softly spoken and friendly locals welcomed us with big smiles.

As we drove through the city, we saw stunning views of the ocean and small roadside shops selling fresh vegetables and colourful clothing.

Women walked by dressed in similar bright patterned dresses, carrying vibrant woollen bags on their shoulders and even with the strap across their forehead allowing the bag to hang down their back!

Men carried baskets as they walked. Some of them were dressed as security guards in front of shopping and gated areas and I was surprised to see so few people in the streets, especially the absence of motorbikes. I loved the chill atmosphere which made the city feel peaceful and unhurried.

Since then, we have never walked in remote villages, but we have travelled from Port Moresby by plane to other parts of the country like Lae, Mount Hagen, Madang, Kokopo and Goroka. Because of the short distances, it takes roughly one hour, and the planes are quite compact.

These planes, locally called "balus", are smaller than the ones you take to go to some of the neighbouring countries like Australia, Philippines, Solomon Islands and Fiji.

They look like buses with wings to me. That's why I call them "flying buses" or "flying PMVs".

Everyone here calls the public buses: PMV, which stands for Public Motor Vehicle.

PMVs are always full of people, with the doors open!

It looks dangerous, but it seems nobody gets hurt.

At the bus stations, PMVs wait to have a minimum of people inside before it moves, so the driver makes sure the trip is worthwhile financially.

Travellers need to leave home with enough time to be at their destination punctually.
PNG
CAL - 204

Groups of people also travel in pickup trucks, cars with an open tray at the back.

What an experience!

I love seeing them smiling at us, feeling the hot air on their faces and being able to see the view of the turquoise ocean.

Papua New Guineans are indeed happy people.

You can also travel by boat.

Banana boats or traditional canoes are used by the local coastal and island people.

You will see lots of beautiful boats at the Port Moresby Harbour.

On the weekends, we enjoy going to some islands like Loloata and Fisherman's Island, where we often see locals with their canoes fishing on pristine water.

On these islands, we often see starfish.

Starfish are amazing creatures.

The first time we saw one we couldn't resist holding it briefly and examining its body, then we carefully returned it to the bottom of the ocean since I heard they die if you keep them out of the water for over two or three minutes. We don't want that to happen!

Did you know that starfish, which is not a fish, can live up to 35 years and can be male, female or hermaphrodite?

Yes, some starfish produce only eggs (female), others only sperm (male) and some of them produce eggs and sperm at the same time.

How fascinating nature is!

If like Papua New Guineans, you are brave and strong enough, you can walk long distances.

We know some fit friends of Daddy and Mummy who have walked the Kokoda Track, a famous 96 km trail through the jungles of Papua New Guinea. Each year, thousands of Australians make a commemorative trek at Kokoda to honour those who served there during World War II.

We also have the privilege of knowing the adventure of Samuel, our swimming coach who walked 400 km from Alatou, Milne Bay to Port Moresby for two months with a friend of his.

Their feet were full of blisters and they could no longer wear shoes.

They had only a pair of thongs they shared, taking turns all the way to Port Moresby.

They crossed rivers, passed through villages and climbed mountains with the advice of other locals to avoid areas with crocodiles.

They climbed trees to get coconut juice and paw paws, they cooked vegetables on the fire and caught some freshwater prawns from the rivers which allowed them to get enough food from nature to get to the capital.

That must have been hard work!

We sometimes complain after 30 minutes of walking asking "Are we there yet?"

There is nothing better than having a goal in life.

"No pain, no gain," my dad says.

3. How did Papua New Guinea get its name?

The name "New Guinea" was created hundreds of years ago, in 1545 by one of the first Europeans to explore the region.

This Spanish explorer noted the resemblance between the landscape and appearance of the local people to those in Equatorial Guinea in Africa.

Apparently, the word papua comes from the Malay word "papuwah" which means "frizzy" or "curly" describing the hair of the local people he encountered.

4. What does Papua New Guinea's flag look like?

In 1971, as PNG was preparing to become an independent country, they held a nationwide competition to design a flag for Papua New Guinea.

Susan Karike, a 15-year-old girl won the competition.

The five stars represent the Southern Cross constellation, which is visible only in the southern hemisphere and carries cultural importance for the nations in that region.

A bird-of-paradise (called Kumul amongst locals) symbolises the cultural vibrancy of the different parts of Papua New Guinea, since the bird's feathers were used by many cultural groups for decoration and adorning traditional attire. The bird of paradise flying above the Southern Cross on the flag also symbolises freedom as PNG emerged as an independent country.

Black, red and yellow are the traditional colours of Papua New Guinea's style of art and clothing.

Clàudia loves to start a game to see who can spot the most flags in Port Moresby — whether we're in the car or at the stadium with Daddy, watching the national rugby league team, the Kumuls – which means "birds of paradise" in Tok Pisin, the local language. Fans wave the PNG flag with pride and often wear jerseys inspired by its vibrant colours. There, it's impossible to keep count!

But the stadium isn't the only place where the flag appears. You can find it everywhere — at school, the airport, Ela Beach market, Parliament House, APEC Haus, and so many more places!

Sometimes I spot more. Sometimes she does.

5. What is the National Emblem?

The national emblem of Papua New Guinea was designed by Hal Holman, an Australian artist and adopted on 1 July 1971.

It consists of a bird-of-paradise over a traditional ceremonial spear and a kundu drum.

Kundu is a pidgin name in Papua New Guinea for an hourglass shaped drum used to accompany formal occasions, religious ceremonies and celebrations.

A **spear** is a stick with a sharp point traditionally used for hunting, fishing, fighting and dancing. Mum bought a wooden carving of the emblem at the craft market, and we keep it in a special place - right on top of the piano. But that's not the only place we see it because the emblem is everywhere!

It appears in PNG passports, on coins and banknotes, on postal stamps, and it is proudly displayed at the National Museum and official buildings.

6. What is the National Anthem?

In 1975, the Englishman Thomas Shacklady won a competition to compose the new PNG National Anthem.

We sing the National Anthem at the beginning of our school assemblies for Independence Day celebrations and other national events.

I love the power of this song, especially when we sing loudly the chorus part:

"We are independent and we are free, Pa-pu-aaaaa New Gui-neeeeeeee!

It brings all of us together.

Every time we sing it at school, I get a bit emotional because I can see how happy and proud Papua New Guineans are of being from Papua New Guinea, and I think this is admirable.

7. How many languages does Papua New Guinea have?

Papua New Guinea is the most linguistically diverse country in the world.

Did you know that there are around 7000 languages in the world and over 800 of them are spoken in PNG?

Yes... over 800 languages.

You heard right.

Unfortunately, some of the Papua Niugini languages are slowly disappearing.

Some native languages are only spoken in the villages with less than 100 speakers.

In most countries, one, two, or three languages are spoken.

In Spain, for example, four languages are spoken: Spanish, Catalan, Gallego and Euskera.

Everybody in Spain speaks Spanish but then, depending on the area they live in, they speak a second language.

So, my sister and I can speak Spanish and Catalan (thanks to our mum's persistence speaking and reading for us in both languages and playing songs and videos in both languages), English (thanks to our dad who is from Australia) and now we are learning Tok Pisin.

We really value languages at home. The more, the better.

This also happens here in PNG.

Papua New Guineans are multilingual people!

Just about everyone speaks Tok Pisin and then, depending on the area people live, they also speak their village language and maybe even the neighbouring village language too.

Most people in the capital also speak English and most of the educational curriculum in PNG primary and secondary schools is delivered in English.

The other three most spoken local languages in PNG are:

- Hiri Motu, in the Gulf Province and the National Capital District
- Enga, in Enga Province (Highland's region)
- Huli, in Hela Province (Highland's region)

How is it possible that the village at the top of the hill speaks a different language than the village on the bottom of the hill? It's hard to believe, but it is true.

8. What is Tok Pisin?

Tok Pisin (literally, "bird talk") is a creole language or a mixed language formed from the contact between local languages and other languages, like Japanese and German but mainly English.

That's why Tok Pisin (called also Pidgin) and English have similar words, but I couldn't really understand them when we first arrived here.

It is not a difficult language to learn if you speak English and try your best to practice.

Would you like to learn some words in pidgin?

ENGLISH	TOK PISIN
GOOD MORNING	MONIN
HOW ARE YOU?	YU ORAIT?
I'M FINE	MI ORAIT TASOL
WHAT IS YOUR NAME?	WANEM NEM BILONG YU?
MY NAME IS JÚLIA	NEM BILONG MI JÚLIA
WHERE ARE YOU FROM?	YU BILONG WANEM HAP?
I'M FROM SPAIN	MI BILONG SPAIN
WOMAN/GIRL	MERI
HOUSEKEEPER	HAUS MERI
LITTLE	LIKLIK
KID	PIKININI
GOODBYE	BAI
GOOD AFTERNOON	AVINUN
SEE YOU LATER	LUKIM YU
WELCOME	WELKAM
THANK YOU VERY MUCH	TENKIU TRU
ALL OF YOU	OLGETA
NO, THANK YOU	SORI NOGUT
OLDER PERSON	BUBU
FOOD	KAIKAI
ONE	WANPLA
TWO	TOOPLA

9. What languages are the official languages in Papua New Guinea?

In PNG there are four official languages: English, Tok Pisin, Hiri Motu and Sign Language.

1. English was the language spoken by the British and Australians that governed PNG before 1975. When PNG became an independent country, the new government kept English as an official language.

2. Tok Pisin called also "Pidgin" is the most widely spoken language throughout Papua New Guinea.

The local news on TV and radio is in Pidgin so every Papua New Guinean can understand.

3. Hiri Motu is the pure language spoken in the surrounding areas of Port Moresby by Motu people, an ethnic group of PNG people. There is a less formal language version of Hiri Motu called Police Motu which came about because of attempts by the region's colonisers and their nonindigenous police agents to communicate in Motu with people in Port Moresby. To give one example: "good morning" in Hiri Motu is "Daba namona" while in Police Motu is "Dabai"

4. Sign language is used by the deaf population throughout the country, although there is not only one but several village sign languages.

Did you know that each country has its own sign language?

Just like different languages are spoken around the world, people who have hearing difficulties use different sign languages depending on where they come from. How cool!

I never thought so until I met our knowledgeable PNG Sign Language teacher at school.

It's estimated there are 130 sign languages around the world.

Just to mention three of them:

In Australia they use AUSLAN, the Australian Sign Language and

In France they use LSF, Langues de Signes Français

In Spain they use SSL, Spanish Sign Language

10. Who are the Wantoks?

When two Papua New Guineans are from the same clan, tribe, area, or speak the same local language, they consider themselves family.

They are called their Wantok (One talk), because they speak the same language.

When a Papua New Guinean needs help, the wantok community is always there to offer a place to sleep, food to eat or even money to send kids to school.

In Papua New Guinea's culture, "sharing" is expected.

They share food, toys, clothes, time, money, houses and often, even the bedroom with their siblings and parents.

Can you believe that sometimes, in the villages, even 20 family members can share the same house?

It must be so much fun!

11. What do people look like in PNG?

Like any other population, PNG's people exhibit a wide range of physical appearances, reflecting the country's rich cultural heritage and the diversity of its population.

So, Papua New Guineans can look many different ways but if you are from there or been there long enough, you can definitely tell the difference in their looks and guess what part of PNG they are from.

Although they do vary from tribe to tribe and valley to valley there are certain facial similarities depending on the area they are originally from.

People on the mainland look different to people from the islands and again, people from the highlands, look different to people from coastal regions.

As an example, people from coastal PNG are light-skinned whereas Bougainvilleans have a very dark-coloured skin.

Tattoos on their body and face also help to know what part of PNG they are from.

Our friend Grace is from East New Britain and all the locals can guess where she is from only looking at her facial traits.

12. What are bilum and bilas?

One of the most iconic garments in Papua New Guinea is the bilum, a woven bag traditionally made from animal fur, tree or plant fibres carried by women and used to transport veggies and wood.

Nowadays, the bilum is commonly used as a ladies' handbag and it can be made from different materials like plastic, colourful wool or, also, natural fibres.

Each part of PNG has its own unique bilum and basket designs for men and women.

PNG people know where other people are from only by looking at their bilum.

I found it amazing seeing women in the street carrying a sleeping baby in their bilums and others carrying a bilum full of veggies on their head.

They must have very strong muscles in their neck.

Auntie Lisa made one for each of us.

They are gorgeous.

We use our bilums to carry our books and toys when we go out, which puts a smile on more than one face.

The smile follows with this sentence: "Ohh Papua New Guinean girls."

Papua New Guineans really love seeing us with the bilum.

Imagine when we wear a Meri Blouse!

Bilas, instead, are the traditional decorative items people wear only at special cultural ceremonies like weddings, sing sings and important events. It reflects the interconnection of people to their place and all its living things (plants and animals). It includes amazing headdresses made of feathers, grass skirts, shell jewelry and face and body paint.

13. How do people dress?

The most common women's dress is called Meri Blouse.

Women in PNG adore all types of Meri Blouses and they use them for different occasions depending on the pattern and fabric. They use a special and beautiful one to go to church. They wear PNG colours when it is time to celebrate the Independence Day, and they choose their favourite colours for an everyday use.

Modern fashion has influenced the way women dress, so you can see women wearing all sorts of dresses, pants, skirts and t-shirts.

Quality clothes can be found in shops and malls, but second-hand shops are my mum's favourite.

Buying second hand clothes is not only good for your pocket, my mum says, but also for the environment.

She often buys clothes for us there.

She is so good at finding similar shirts for us so we can match.

We have our own style, but we like matching clothes.

The day we really love wearing a Meri Blouse is for Independence Day.

That day... we are called again:
"Ohh Papua New Guinean girls," with a smile on their faces.
They are proud we embrace their culture.
We are blessed to feel so welcomed.
We love PNG.

14. What are the main religions and beliefs in Papua New Guinea?

Papua New Guinean people have well established Indigenous belief systems and traditions. There are many Indigenous groups in PNG and they have their own way of connecting to nature, their own explanations about the origin of the universe, their own oral stories, myths and legends, their own healing practices.

A common Indigenous tradition is that rituals are necessary for a person's spiritual and physical well-being.

As an example, in the Sepik area the crocodile is worshiped and believed to be the ancestor of humans. In some Sepik villages, people have a ritual where boys are given marks on their body (scars) that look like a crocodile's skin.

In Milne Bay, it is believed that if you disrespect nature a bad storm will appear to show that the spirits are angry with this behaviour.

Christianity was introduced to PNG by European missionaries during the 1800s.

Nowadays, the Papua New Guinean population is predominantly Christian and people go to Church on Sundays or on Saturdays if they are Seventh-day Adventists.

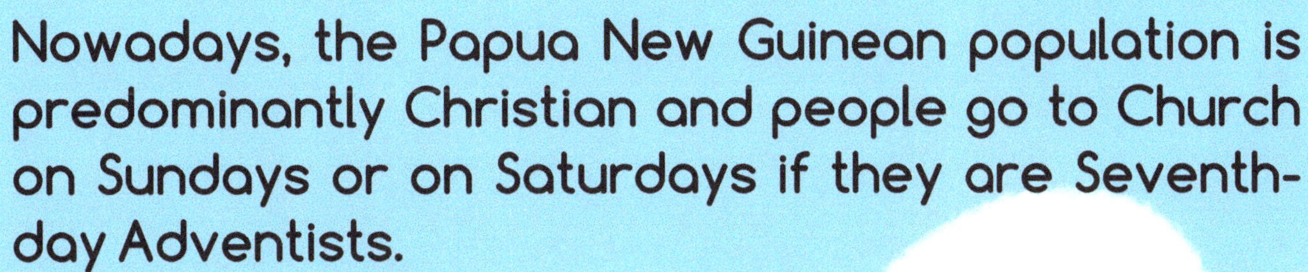

Many PNG people seem to live their lives by combining their Indigenous beliefs and traditions with the Christian religion.

We used to ask Dad why different religions have different Gods, and which is the real one.

We now understand that depending on where you are born and what your parents and ancestors believed in, you will probably follow certain beliefs and religion.

We feel lucky to have been exposed to different religions and to learn from all of them, but we choose to stick to none.

15. How do PNG parents name their kids when they are born?

Since PNG is considered a Christian nation, some parents may choose to call their kids: Grace, Faith, Mary, Hope, Lucy if they have a baby girl.

Joseph, Andrew, Gabriel, Paul, Thomas, Vincent, Zachariah if they have a baby boy.

Other parents prefer to choose names after a family member, after someone they admire or appreciate, after a village's name or after some things we can find in nature.

Our friend Lahara for example, is named after a type of wind in PNG in Motuan language. Before giving this name to their daughter, her parents asked for a blessing from a senior person amongst Motuans. It is culturally important and a sign of respect to do so when you are from PNG and use another people's language.

Our friend Kaibadi is named after a village's name that means "special spear" used for ocean diving and made of black palm. This name was chosen to honour his grandfather who dedicated his life to raising community awareness about ocean safety and promoting micro-businesses among fishermen.

I learnt from my Indian friend Niranjana that her name is associated with a Hindu goddess and it means "night of the full moon".

Our Haus Meri, Lisa, named her son after our wonderful dad, Andy.

Can you believe it?

When Lisa told us that she would name her son Andy, we thought for a moment that she was joking.

Not long after, we learnt that this is a quite common practice in PNG.

Then, sometimes, this person becomes the godfather or godmother of the child with financial responsibilities.

We felt honoured to know that Lisa appreciates us to the point of naming her son after our dad.

Every parent has different reasons for choosing a particular name.

Sometimes even other members of the community can choose or help to choose the name of a baby.

How interesting!

Who selected your name?

Do you know the meaning of your name?

16. Why can PNG people call mummy, sister or auntie to more than one woman?

Lisa, our kind, responsible and hard-working haus meri is from the Highlands.

We call Lisa, auntie Lisa, since we love her so much and she loves us as if she was our second mum.

Sometimes we even call her mummy Lisa.

When our birth mum heard us calling her "mummy Lisa" she had to think twice and decide whether to suggest us not to call her mummy or let us do it.

At the beginning, our mum didn't like sharing this honoured title with another person. We heard her saying... I had to wait 40 years to become a mum and now...

Do I have to share this beautiful and unique title?

She is very proud of being our mum and in our culture, generally speaking, there is only one mum.

Mum did some research about Indigenous People Worldviews versus Western Worldviews and then let us call Lisa, mummy Lisa. After all, mum wanted to respect PNG culture and Lisa was taking care of us like a second mum.

If you would like to have a better understanding of how Indigenous People understand the world, or how they explain their identity, beliefs and collective culture, I suggest you do some research too with your parents and your teachers!

It is fascinating how the world can be seen so differently at all levels depending on your culture, especially if the culture is collective (like in PNG) or individual (like in Western countries).

Mum embraced the Papua New Guinean culture where the concept of family extends beyond just biological relatives to include community members, neighbours and friends.

This is why we call Daddy's friend Sean, uncle Sean, and Daddy's friend Paul, uncle Paul, even if they are not our uncles.

PNG people call sister, brother and other family titles to other people even though they are not family members. It is a way of showing respect, warmth, solidarity, inclusivity, hospitality and a sense of shared identity and belonging.

17. How are houses built?

Architecture in Papua New Guinea varies from region to region adapted for climate, landscape and materials.

Each structure has a distinct purpose, whether for living, community gatherings, spiritual rituals, or warfare.

Domestic dwellings were traditionally made with timber, bamboo, coconut and sago palm leaves, amongst other materials, and often built on stilts over land or water.

In every village in the Trobriand Islands, you can find some Yam houses where yams are stored after harvesting. I think yams look like sweet potatoes.

The biggest Yam house belongs to the chief and is decorated with paint and shells.

Yams are very important not only as food but also as a symbol of wealth, power, and prosperity. After the harvest, Yam houses are filled with yams and there are big festivities.

The Motu village built over the waters of Moresby Harbour in Port Moresby is fascinating.

We can see it from our balcony.

It is called Hanuabada Village.

18. What are the main cultural festivals throughout the year?

PNG has an incredible and fascinating cultural diversity.

Each tribe gathers to celebrate through rituals and ceremonial dance, music and drama.

They wear costumes and body adornments made of natural fibres and animal skin or fur. They paint their body, put shell jewellery on and use artifacts like the Kundu drum and the spear to dramatise the story that is being told.

This way of telling stories through songs and dances is called 'sing sing'.

PNG is a place of living and flourishing traditions with huge annual festivals.

The 'Goroka Show' is a significant cultural event in the Highlands region of Papua New Guinea and is also the longest running annual cultural festival drawing many tourists to the country every year in September during the weekend closest to the nation's Independence Day celebrations.

Definitely, the most important celebration as a whole country is in September, on the 16th, when we celebrate our Independence Day.

PNG became an independent country from Australia in 1975 and since then, on that week, the entire country is covered with flags. People wear their colours: black, red and yellow and festivals, shows and dances are taking place everywhere.

PNG people are very patriotic and incredibly proud of their independence!

Even at school, each class dresses up and performs dances representing different provinces in front of all the parents.

We put on a show that really needs a team effort.

The whole school community contributes, making the day the most special day of the year.

When I was four years old, I was terrified of the Mud Men, but now, it is the day I love the most.

The independence spirit makes everyone joyful and happy.

There are many other festivals such as:

- Kenu & Kundu Festival (Milne Bay)

- Hiri Moale (Port Moresby)

- Morobe Show (Lae)

- Frangipani Festival (Rabaul)

- Goroka Show (Goroka)

- Crocodile Festival (Wewak)

- Mount Hagen Show (Mount Hagen)

- Mask Festival (Kokopo)

19. How do PNG people get married?

Marriage in Papua New Guinea can be in the world-wide tradition of marriage by a religious or a civil marriage ceremony.

In traditional weddings people wear customary attire with outfits made of tapa cloth, grass skirts and feathers. Clàudia and I would have loved to go to a wedding but we have only seen photos of one celebrated in the Nature Park. The bride was wearing a modern Western attire but traditional dances and songs were performed to celebrated the union.

In some PNG families, the tradition of "Bride Price" is still prevalent.

The groom's family pays the bride price but the family of the bride have to agree on what is being paid. The families of the bride and groom meet and have negotiations which can last for weeks or even months. The bride price can be anything from money to livestock (cows, chickens, pigs, etc) and goods such as four-wheel drive cars. If the bride price is not paid, the wedding can be cancelled.

My dad often gets jokes that he will be richer when my sister and I get married in PNG since, as daughters, our future husbands' family would have to pay a bride price to ours.

I don`t find it funny but controversial. Aren't we equal partners in marriage? Why do they need to pay for us? I will have time to think about it, but in any case, it's not something that will happen anytime soon, if it ever happens.

20. How do they honour and bury their dead people?

When a loved one is lost in PNG, not only do immediate relatives mourn the deceased but so do the extended family and friends who travel from near and far to the "haus krai" which translates to house of crying.

Everyone gives support to the mourning family by bringing some money, prepared dishes or other food items such as rice, flour, sugar, milk, tea bags, coffee, bread, fruits and veggies, tinned food and fresh meat.

The ritual of "Haus Krai" represents an immense emotional an economical support.

Visitors make sure the family knows they are not alone in this difficult situation, that lots of people care for them and that there is always someone to talk to.

They talk to remember the dead person; they sing together and they cry.

My dad went to a Haus Krai once and he said people cried a lot and loud.

It is their way of expressing their sadness.

After some days or even weeks during which the body is prepared in a funeral home for burial, so there are no bad smells, they do the funeral in the church where ladies are expected to wear black clothes and cut their hair short and men are expected to grow their hair and beard.

After the funeral the deceased body is returned to their native land to be buried.

Can you guess how the body is transported if its native land is in another PNG city or village?

You guessed well... by plane.

21. What's Papua New Guinea economy based on?

Papua New Guinea is one of the world's least developed countries that works together with companies and NGOs to improve their healthcare system, water access and sanitation, civil unrest and education.

Although PNG is rich in natural resources, it faces major socioeconomic challenges.

Mining is an important part of the economy holding deposits of oil, gas, gold and copper.

However, most rural people are subsistence farmers, which means that they have animals or crops that provide food to support their family – this includes fishing and cultivating fruits and vegetables like mangos, pineapples, pawpaw, bananas, taro, yams, sago, rice, cassava and sweet potatoes.

The main crops PNG export, which means sold to other countries are: coffee, cocoa, vanilla, tea, palm oil and coconuts.

Did you know that coffee, chocolate and vanilla come from beans? I love watching videos about how chocolate and vanilla are produced, since they are my favourite flavours.

What ice-cream do you prefer?

Chocolate or vanilla?

Craft Markets, Vegetable Markets and Fish Markets are a big part of PNG's economy too.

On the weekends, we like to go to the Craft Markets where a mix of traditional and contemporary art and crafts from Papua New Guinea are sold, from fashion to home, décor, food and souvenirs.

There, we bought a beautiful painting for my dad's birthday with lots of hidden sea animals.

Every time we look at it, we see a new one.

Local artists in PNG are so talented!

There is also a fresh fish local market called Koki Market where shells, lobsters, prawns, octopus, squid and different types of fish try to escape from their baskets. That's how fresh everything is there.

On Fridays, my mum likes to buy vegetables at Boroko local market.

Everything is so fresh too and the variety of fruits and veggies is great.

The vendor's smile makes my mum's day.

The only fruit she can't forget to buy for us is… coconut!

Well… and we also ask for Papaya, bananas and mangos… we love fruit!

But what Mum can't really forget to buy when it is in season is the delicious crunchy galip nut.

We love having it after school, in the car, on the way to gymnastics, as a healthy snack.

Have you ever tried it?

22. What is the currency?

The official currency in Papua New Guinea, is the Kina which is abbreviated to the currency code PGK (Papua New Guinea Kina).

1 Kina is divided into 100 cents or toea (which means shell in a local language).

There are notes of 2 Kina, 5 Kina, 10 Kina, 20 Kina, 50 Kina, and 100 Kina.

If you look closer, you will see beautiful drawings on these notes: birds of paradise, spears, carved "hourglass" drums, the parliament building, the Prime Minister Michael Somare and more.

You might even be lucky enough to see a K50 or K100 banknote, launched in 2025, to celebrate PNG's 50 years of independence.

10
Bank of Papua New Guinea
10

20
Bank of Papua New Guinea

5
Bank of Papua New Guinea
5

Bank of Papua New Guinea
50

The word Kina refers to a type of shell used by early Papua New Guinea civilisation as money.

'Kina shells' is the name for these crescent-shaped cut and polished clam shells prized for their golden yellow colour.

Men and women wear Kina shell necklaces.

Papua New Guinea's money is still called Kina after these shells.

Kina shells are rare treasures from Papua New Guinea and a sign of wealth.

I found it fascinating how Kina shells were historically used in PNG.

These shells were used for trade, bride price and other transactions.

Can you imagine exchanging several pigs for a large Kina shell?

Can you imagine buying a canoe or land with shells?

Yeah…that's how they did it.

No money was involved.

23. What type of government rules the country?

Papua New Guinea is a member of the Commonwealth of Nations.

The Commonwealth is an international association of 56 member states that have no legal obligations to one another but are connected through their use of the English language and historical-cultural ties.

The British monarch rules over PNG since it is part of the Commonwealth.

In PNG, the monarch is represented by a Governor-General while the Prime Minister is the leader of the political party elected by the people to run the country.

Sir Michael Thomas Somare (1936 -2021) was a Papua New Guinean politician.

He was the first Prime Minister after independence, widely called the "father of the nation" (Tok Pisin: papa blo kantri).

24. How has PNG gone in the Commonwealth Games?

PNG has taken part in the Olympic Games since 1976, but the nation has never won a medal. However, have you heard about the Commonwealth Games?

The Commonwealth Games is an international multi-sport competition that lasts approximately ten days and it is held every four years in different countries.

These games are like the Olympic Games, but instead of having athletes from around the world, only the countries that are part of the Commonwealth of Nations can compete.

PNG has participated since 1962 and since then, has won several medals in weightlifting, boxing, lawn bowls, swimming and shooting.

NAME	GAMES	SPORT	EVENT
GEUA TAU	1990 AUCKLAND	LAWN BOWLS	WOMEN'S SINGLES
RYAN PINI	2006 MELBOURNE	SWIMMING	MEN'S 100 M. BUTTERFLY
DIKA TOUA	2014 GASGOW	WEIGHTLIFTING	WOMEN'S 53 KG
STEVEN KARI	2014 GLASGOW	WEIGHTLIFTING	MEN'S 94 KG
STEVEN KARI	2018 GOLD COAST	WEIGHTLIFTING	MEN'S 94 KG

In this table you can see the Gold medals and these are the winners in action.

Great achievements!

Do you know when and where the next Commonwealth Games are going to be celebrated?

25. What's the weather like in PNG?

In the coastal regions the climate is warm or very hot the whole year and there are only two seasons: wet and dry.

In Port Moresby during the dry months (May to October) it is windy, hot and doesn't rain much. The rest of the year is also hot, but it rains almost every day, which makes the climate so uncomfortably hot.

If you go up to the mountains in the Highlands regions, make sure you take your jumper because the high altitude brings cooler weather all year around, especially at night.

If during the dry season you dare to climb up to 4,509 metres to the summit of PNG's highest volcanic mountain called Mount Wilhelm, you can probably touch frost.

Snowfall in tropical regions is rare, but... it happens.

Can you place in a map some other mountains around the Equator where you can find snow?

There is one in Indonesia, another one in the Philippines, in Tanzania, in The Andes mountains and in Ecuador, just to mention some.

Geography fascinates me.

26. How does mother nature treat PNG? Volcanos and Earthquakes

PNG has the potential for natural disasters since it is prey to volcanic activity, earthquakes and tidal waves.

Papua New Guinea sits on the Pacific "Ring of Fire" where much of the world's earthquake and volcanic activities occur, especially on the eastern edge of PNG.

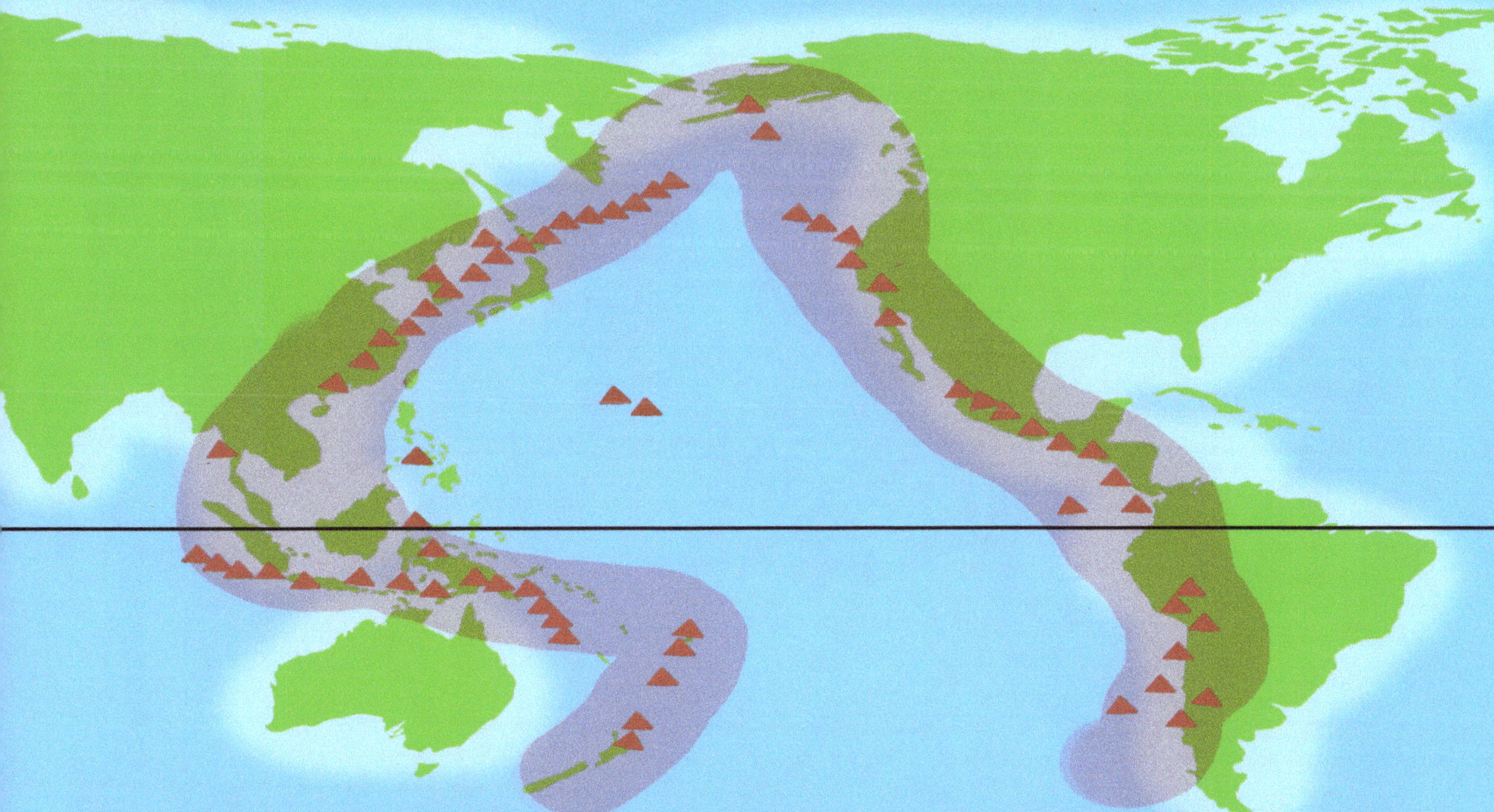

So, when you are in the capital, be prepared for some earth movements.

Sometimes, my sister Clàudia and I get a bit scared but most of the time, we don't even notice it because usually the epicenter of the earthquake is miles away.

When there is an earthquake mummy plays "Elegy for the Victims of the Earthquake and Tsunami" on the piano for us after dinner in honour of all the victims of natural disasters.

It is a moment to relax, remembering those who suffer and be thankful for being safe.

This is an emotional song.

Mum even cries while playing it, like its composer did in a concert. Did you know he is blind, but he can look straight into people's hearts through his music?

While Daddy's country, Australia, is the only continent in the world without an active volcano, PNG has at least 20 volcanoes, yes... you read that correctly... 20.

We visited one volcano in Kokopo, New Britain, called the Vulcan volcano and there we learnt about the catastrophe that took place in 1994.

A twin volcanic eruption buried Rabaul, a town in Papua New Guinea once known as the "pearl of the Pacific". It was the second time in 57 years that eruptions had destroyed the town.

But this one is not the only unfortunate volcano eruption.

The explosion of Mount Lamington volcano in 1951 was much worse.

It destroyed more than 200 km² of dense tropical rainforest and killed approximately 3000 people.

Volcanoes have the habit of sleeping and being quiet long enough for people to forget the danger they represent. I have to admit that this is a bit scary.

Have you heard about the lost city of Pompeii?

Pompeii was a city with about 10,000 residents, in the south of Italy that was buried in ash and other volcanic debris when Mount Vesuvius erupted about 2000 years ago.

It happened almost overnight, and its ruins were discovered only in 1748, after 1500 years.

I admire the patience and work of archeologists finding out how people used to live in Pompeii.

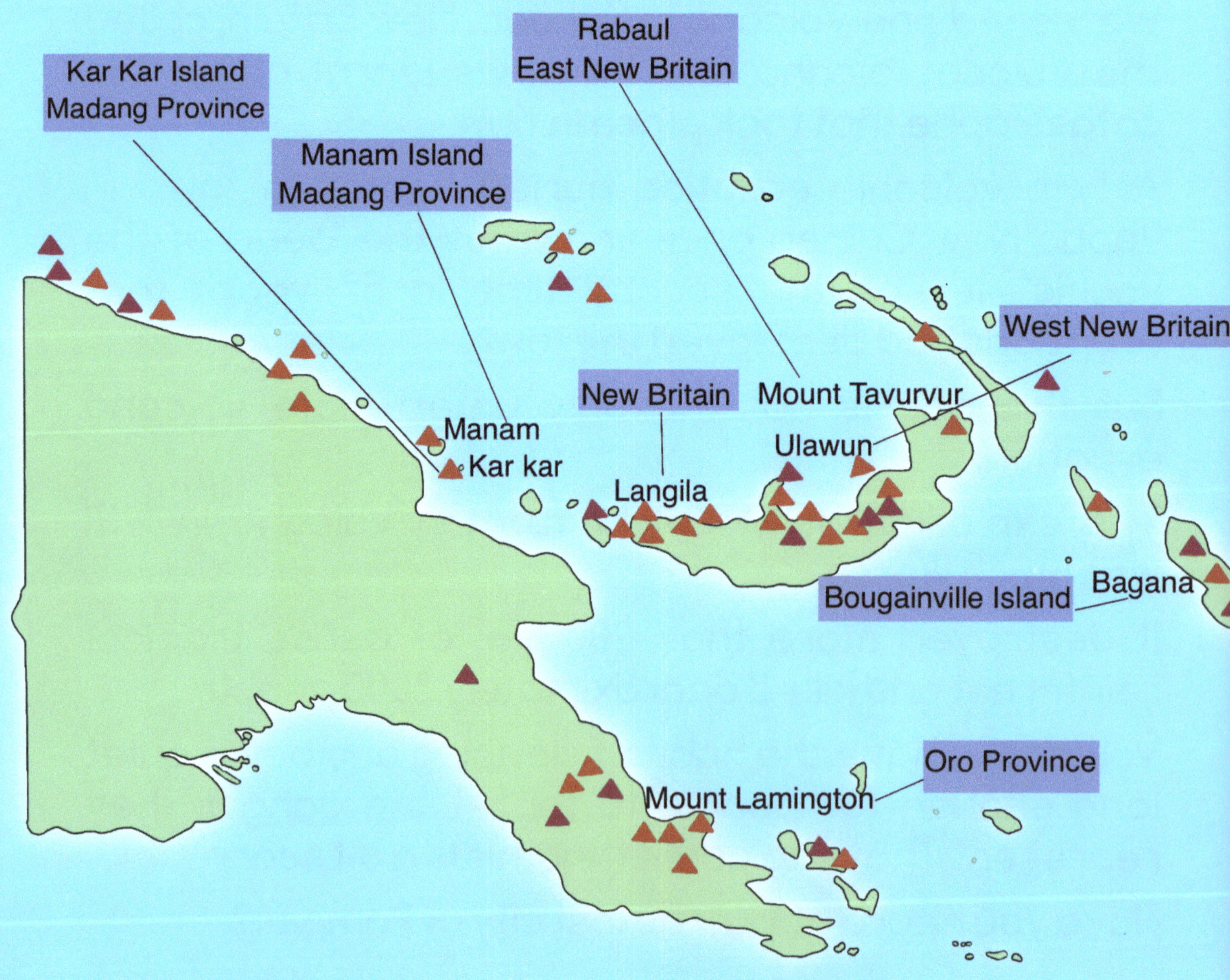

27. Would you like to know my favourite animals from Papua New Guinea?

There are hundreds of animals in PNG that are endemic to the country, which means they can only be found in PNG. Some of them are endangered and need to be preserved to avoid extinction.

Nature Park in Waigani Drive in Port Moresby is doing a great job in wildlife conservation, preservation and research.

We love going there on the weekends and explore around, especially to see the snakes, the tree kangaroos and talk to the cockatoos.

Can you believe they answer back?

Just kidding, they only say "Hellooo" but it is fun and they love a gentle pet on their head!

Would you like to try?

Let's meet some of my favourite PNG animals:

Blue-eyed cockatoo is a large white bird with a mobile crest, a black beak, and a light blue rim of featherless skin around each eye that gives this species its name.

Matschie's Tree kangaroo: The beautiful fur is used for traditional decoration and is hunted for food by the local communities.

Emperor Bird of Paradise: Males and females are slightly different. Males have a green face and throat and very long white tail feathers. In the mating display, the males hang upside-down on the branch and spread their white plumage. The females have more brown feathers.

Dwarf Cassowary: Is the largest native vertebrate. It communicates with other cassowaries using a low booming sound.

Echidnas: These egg-laying mammals have a long beak and prefer living in areas with no human presence. It uses its unique beak to search for earthworms and other invertebrates in the soil. They also have a poisonous claw to deter predators.

Forest Wallabies are shy and difficult to observe. They prefer living in large grassland areas up in the mountains.

Scheepmaker's crowned pigeon: is a large terrestrial pigeon that has a bluish-grey plumage with elaborate blue lacy crests, red iris and a deep maroon breast. Both sexes have a similar appearance.

28. What is diving and snorkelling like in PNG?

Due to the three major seas currents meeting at this country's waterside, the biodiversity here is spectacular and cannot be found like this anywhere else in the world.

Mum dives but dad and us only snorkel.

You don't need to go deep into the water to be amazed by nature here.

Fish and coral colours are seen with fantastic water clarity.

While snorkelling you can see turtles, moray eels, clownfish (or Nemos, as you would probably know them), rare Rhinopia, mantas, schools of barracuda and you can get up close to reef gardens where nudibranchs can be spotted.

I will always remember the day my sister Clàudia and I saw our first sea turtle. We were swimming in the deep ocean, holding hands to ease our fear of the vast clear water underneath us when I spotted her in the distance. I squeezed Clàudia's hand to get her attention and pointed at the turtle.

She was majestic.

She looked at me straight in my eyes before gracefully swimming away.

We felt like the luckiest girls in the world!

29. Would you like to know my favourite trees and flowers from Papua New Guinea?

You will see in PNG some of the biggest trees you have ever seen.

In the capital, the biggest trees are called rain trees but you can also find pine trees, mango trees, paw-paw trees, banana trees, coconut trees and moringa trees.

Have you ever seen a banana tree? Well first of all, apparently the banana tree is not a tree but a plant. However, what I was surprised the most with was when I saw that the bananas grow upwards.

Did you know that?

I still can't believe it. It looks like bananas are going against gravity. Cherries, pears, peaches and any other fruit I know is like an earring to a branch, always looking down.

Nature will never stop astonishing me.

Heliconias and orchids are two of my favourite flowers grown here.

Our family in Spain appreciate us sending them our photos with different types of flowers especially these tropical ones.

All my family love flowers and we have been inspired to do so too.

People here use coconut leaves and moringa leaves to cook with or wrap food, but local grandmas make medicine from moringa leaves too. They boil them and offer the drink to anyone who feels sick in the family. Grandmas also boil lemongrass and other leaves and herbs to help with colds and offer to steam or inhale its hot vapor.

My favourite medicine for colds is when mum boils ginger in hot water, adds a squeezed lemon and some honey from the Highlands.

It is delicious and works wonders.

30. What are some of Papua New Guinea's traditional vegetables and cooking methods?

Some Saturdays, mum takes us to Boroko market.

This is where we buy all our fruits and vegetables.

The vendors call out:

Would you like to buy yams, taro, kaukau (sweet potato), sago, bananas or maybe you'd like some sugarcane?

Not only are the vegetables different from other countries, the people of PNG use different cooking methods.

The method that I find most fascinating is a Mumu.

A Mumu is an earth oven.

A big hole is dug in the ground and filled with lots of hot coals or stones.

Then, meat and vegetables wrapped with banana leaves are placed on top or around the stones so the food cooks in the hole.

It takes a really long time so you can't be in a hurry if you are having a Mumu, especially if you start the process by killing a pig, one of the most valuable possessions in PNG.

It's time to say goodbye.

I hope you enjoyed reading this book, and you learnt lots.

Your parents might have learnt something too.

Mum says that learning is a lifelong process and that we don't stop learning throughout life.

Dad teaches us to be thankful for the good things in life and to make the most of it.

Living in Papua New Guinea has influenced the way we see the world now.

It has given us the opportunity to get to know local kids and other kids from around the world which I think has put us on the track to becoming citizens of the world.

From wherever you are reading me, I trust you are making the most of every day and experience joy in the big and small moments.

I have to admit that I am not always happy... but at home we try to celebrate simple efforts and achievements.

Today, we celebrate that you have read with us.

GLOSSARY, Mini-dictionary to help you understand words from this book.

Airstrip: It is like a road for airplanes, a simple and small runway where airplanes take off and land.

Anthem: It is a special song that people sing to show love for their country, group, or a big idea. For example, people stand and sing their national anthem to represent their country before a big game, especially when teams from different nations are playing.

Archipelago: A group of islands that are close together.

Banana Boat: There are two types. The inflatable ones and the motorised ones. This last one is the type of boat used in PNG for transportation and travel between islands. And... if you wonder, they don't look like a banana.

Cassava: It is a tropical root vegetable and a major source of carbohydrates in many parts of the world, especially in Africa, South America, and Southeast Asia. It is also known as yuca or manioc. Cassava is processed into various products, such as tapioca and cassava flour.

Commonwealth of Nations: The Commonwealth of Nations, often called the Commonwealth, is a political association of 56 member countries, most of which were former territories of the British Empire. Each country is independent but shares historical ties with the British Empire and follows Commonwealth values like democracy, human rights, and trade cooperation. PNG joined in 1975 (after independence from Australia) and still recognizes the British monarch as its head of state, represented by a Governor-General.

PNG participates in the major sporting event called **Commonwealth Games**, scholarships, and development programs.

Dreaded question: It is a question that makes someone feel nervous or uneasy. It means something that is **feared** or **worried about** because it is unpleasant or scary.

Eastern part of the island: the east part of the island, the right side of the island looking at the world map. If you are facing north, the east is to your right and the west to your left. So **the western** part of the island is on the left side.

Emblem: It is a special picture, symbol, or sign that represents a group, a team, or an idea. For example, a school might have an emblem on its uniforms, or a superhero might have a special emblem on their costume.

Expatriate, expat for short: It is a person who lives in a country that is not their own, usually for work, school, political or personal reasons. Other terms for people living in a different country include: **Immigrants** – People who move intending to stay permanently in the new another country. **Refugees** – People forced to leave their country due to danger. **Tourists/Visitors** – People staying for a short time in a new country. Some immigrants move again, either to another country or back to their home country. Expatriates usually move temporarily and might not plan to stay forever. However, sometimes, expats end up staying permanently and becoming immigrants or even citizens! It's not always a strict definition since people's situations change.

Fraternal twins: Twins who come from two different eggs and can look different or even be a boy and a girl. They can look similar, just like regular siblings, but they don't always. Since they come from two different eggs fertilised by two different sperm, they have different DNA—just like any other brothers or sisters.

Galip Nut: It is a nut rich in oil, protein and antioxidants produced by trees native to the Pacific Islands, particularly Papua New Guinea, Solomon Islands, and Vanuatu. Galip nuts are often compared to macadamia nuts in taste and texture. They can be eaten raw, roasted, or processed into oil for cooking and skincare.

Hermaphrodite: Animal or plant that has both boy and girl parts for reproduction so they can reproduce by themselves.

Identical twins: Twins who come from the same fertilized egg, which splits into two. This means they have the exact same DNA and usually look very much alike. They are always the same gender (either both boys or both girls). They are like natural copies of each other.

Incredibly: amazingly, unbelievably, extremely, extraordinarily and remarkably could be synonyms depending on the context.

Indigenous worldview versus Western worldview.

Indigenous worldview sees everything as connected, like a big family. People, animals, and nature all depend on each other, and it's important to respect and care for them. Stories and traditions help people learn. Grandparents and elders tell stories to teach important lessons. **Practical example:** An Indigenous person might see the tree as a **relative** - something that gives shade, food, and air to breathe. They believe the tree has a spirit and should be respected. If they need wood, they take only what they need and thank the tree. They see themselves as part of nature, not separate from it.

Western worldview likes to organize things into categories and study how they work. People focus on learning through books, science, and new ideas.

They believe in progress and changing things to make life better. They believe people should use nature to make life better, like building big cities and machines. Neither way is right or wrong — they are just different! Some people mix both ways to respect nature while also using science to solve problems. Practical example: A Western thinker might see the tree as a resource — something useful for making paper, houses, or furniture. They study how it grows, how to plant more, and how to use it efficiently. They believe humans are in charge of nature and should use it to improve their lives.

Kokoda Track: Famous walking trail in PNG. It is about 96km long and goes through jungles and mountains. People nowadays hike the track to test their strength, Commemorate the soldiers and PNG people who fought there during World War II.

Mainland: Largest land of a country not including its islands.

Malay: It is a language called "Bahasa Melayu", spoken in Malaysia, Indonesia, Brunei, Singapore and parts of Thailand and the Philippines. It is a relatively easy language to learn because it has no verb tenses, so you can use the same word for an action in the past, present and future. The only thing you need to do is add a "time word" to show when the action happened, like: "already" or "will".

Mourn: to feel very sad because someone has died or something important is lost. People mourn by crying, remembering good times, or showing their sadness in different ways. Synonyms: grieve, lament, weep, sorrow, and bewail.

Province: Part of a country. Dividing a country into provinces makes it easier to manage.

Remarkably: extraordinarily, exceptionally, notably, amazingly and surprisingly, could be synonyms depending on the context.

Ring of Fire: It is an area around the edges of the Pacific Ocean. It is home to 75% of the world's active volcanoes (about 450 volcanoes) and around 90% of the world's earthquakes happen there. The region is also prone to tsunamis, which happen when underwater earthquakes, landslides or volcanic eruptions displace large amounts of water. PNG is in the ring of fire so experiences earthquakes almost daily and some with magnitude seven point five or even eight have been catastrophic. PNG's deadliest earthquake is the one that caused the biggest tsunami, off the coast of Aitape, a town in the West Sepik Province in 1998. PNG's most active volcanos are: **Tavurvur** in East New Britain which destroyed Rabaul town in 1994 and the capital was forced to move to Kokopo. **Ulawun** in West New Britain with its major eruptions in 1980 and 2019. **Manam** in Madang Province with major eruptions in 2004/2005. **Kadovar** in East Sepik, dormant for centuries, but suddenly erupted in 2018. **Bagana** in Bougainville with constant lava flows and ash. PNG or any other country cannot predict exactly when the next earthquake will occur however, the Port Moresby Geophysical Observatory monitors seismic activity together with other international organizations.

Sago: It is a starch extracted from the spongy centre of certain tropical palm trees. It is a staple food in parts of Southeast Asia and the Pacific, often processed into flour and cakes. Sago is commonly used in puddings, porridge, and soups. It is rich in carbohydrates but has little protein, vitamins, or minerals. Sago is sometimes confused with tapioca, which comes from cassava, but they are different starch sources.

School of fish: Fish stay in schools or big groups because it helps them survive and **stay safe** (a big group makes it harder for predators to catch one fish), **find food** (if one fish finds food, the others can eat too!), **save energy** (swimming together makes it easier to move) and **travel together** (schools help fish find their way when they move long distances).

Southern Cross constellation: It is a group of stars that can be seen perfectly from countries in the Southern Hemisphere, like Australia, Papua New Guinea, New Caledonia, New Zealand and South America. It is not visible from most of North America, Europe and northern Asia. The flags of Australia, New Zealand and Papua New Guinea have the Southern Cross on them. If you are in one of these countries, just look up at night.

Starchy food: refers to something that contains or is rich in starch, a type of carbohydrate found in many plants. Starchy foods, like potatoes, rice, taro, and bread, provide energy because starch breaks down into sugars during digestion. Starch gives foods a soft or slightly sticky texture when cooked.

Subsistence farmers: Farmers who grow just enough food to feed themselves and their families. They do not usually grow extra food to sell. Their goal is to survive rather than make a profit.

Taro: It is a tropical plant grown for its edible starchy corm (underground stem) and leaves. It is a staple food in many cultures, especially in the Pacific Islands, Southeast Asia, and Africa. Taro is rich in fibre, vitamins, and minerals.

Third culture kids: Children who grow up in a culture different from their parents' home country.

They usually move between countries because of their parents' jobs, like diplomats, military families, or international business workers. Why are they called Third culture kids? Their First culture is considering their parents' home country (where their family is from). Their Second culture refers to the country (or countries) they grow up in. The Third culture is a mix of both, creating their own unique identity. TCKs often speak multiple languages, adapt easily to new places, and feel at home in many cultures—but they may also struggle with where they truly "belong."

Volcanic debris: It refers to rocks, ash, lava fragments, and other materials ejected from a volcano during an eruption. Volcanic debris can be dangerous, covering large areas, damaging buildings, and affecting the environment.

World War II: One of the most important events in history. It was a big war that happened from 1939 to 1945 and involved many countries. Germany, led by Adolf Hitler wanted more land and power. Japan wanted to control more parts of Asia and the Pacific. The Allies were countries like USA, UK, Soviet Union, China and Australia. Many battles were fought in Europe, Asia and the Pacific. One of the battles happened in the Kokoda Track (July-November 1942) where Australian soldiers and Papua New Guineans fought hard against Japanese forces, who wanted to capture Port Moresby to attack Australia. After months of fighting, the Japanese gave up that fight which was a big victory because it stopped Japan from invading Port Moresby and possibly Australia.

Yam: It is a root vegetable similar to sweet potatoes but less sweet, drier and more fibrous. It is an important food crop in many tropical regions like PNG, West Africa and the Caribbean. However, in PNG they are not just food but hold cultural and ceremonial significance. In some communities like the Trobriand Islands it is often associated with status, wealth and social exchange.

Words in Tok Pisin included in this book

Balus: It means airplane or aircraft. It comes from the English word "balloon", which was originally used to describe flying objects. Today, "balus" is the common Tok Pisin word for planes.

Bilas: It means decoration or adornment. It refers to the colourful body paint, jewellery, feathers, shells, and other ornaments worn during special ceremonies, dances, and cultural events. Bilas is an important part of PNG traditions, showing identity, status, and celebration.

Bilum: It is a traditional woven bag from PNG. It is made from plant fibres or wool and is used to carry everything from food and goods to babies. Bilums are important in PNG culture and are often handmade with colourful patterns.

Bride Price: It is the payment such as land, property, money, livestock, or a commercial asset paid by the groom (or his family) to the bride's family. This is common in many African, Asian, and Pacific cultures, including PNG. It is often seen as compensation for the loss of the daughter and recognition of her value to the family. It is part of the marriage process and it has historically been an important element of marriage systems in patrilineal societies. However, not all PNG clans are patrilineal and patriarchal. PNG has over 800 languages and thousands of distinct clans, meaning social structures vary widely.

Many clans in Highland regions and other parts of PNG follow patrilineal systems, where family name, land, and leadership pass through the male line.

In these societies, men hold most decision-making power, and bride price is common.

Some coastal and island communities, such as the Tolai (East New Britain) and Trobriand Islanders (Milne Bay Province), have **matrilineal systems**. This means land and inheritance pass through the mother's lineage, though men may still hold political or ceremonial authority. In these areas, the groom's family may give gifts to show commitment, but this is not the same as a full bride price seen in patrilineal communities. Just as a curiosity, you might like to know about the opposite concept of Bride Price, which is called dowry. It is when the bride's family gives money, goods, or property to the groom (or his family). This practice is common in South Asia, parts of the Middle East, and historically in Europe. It can be a way to help the bride financially in her new home or to strengthen family alliances. So, as you can see, there are multiples ways of approaching marriage.

Hanuabada Village: It means "Big Village" in the Motu language. It is one of the largest and oldest Motuan villages in Port Moresby, known for its stilt, closely packed houses built over the sea. Hanuabada remains as an important symbol of PNG's cultural heritage. It is known for proudly preserving Motu Koita traditions, including language, dance and ceremonies. Its people have a strong sense of community.

Haus Krai: It is a traditional mourning gathering held after someone passes away. It means "house of crying" or "mourning house". It is a significant cultural practice across many PNG communities, blending traditional customs with Christian influences. When someone dies, relatives, friends and community gather for days or even weeks to mourn, pray, support the family and pay respects to the deceased before the final burial or mourning ceremony. People cry, wail, and sometimes engage in rituals such as face-painting, cutting hair, or wearing mourning attire.

Attendees bring food, money, and gifts to help the grieving family, as death-related expenses can be a heavy burden.

Haus Meri: Literally means "house woman" and refers to a woman who works in the home, doing tasks like childcare, cleaning and cooking. It's a common term for domestic workers in PNG. There is another meaning of this word that refers to a safe house that provides protection and support for woman escaping domestic violence, abuse or other dangerous situations.

Kaukau: It means sweet potato. It is one of the staple foods in PNG and main source of carbohydrates for many Papua New Guineas. It is widely grown in the highlands and other regions. Inside it can be purple, orange or white.

Kumul: It means Bird of Paradise, which is the national bird of PNG. The Raggiana Bird of Paradise is an important symbol in PNG, appearing on the national emblem, currency, and even the national airline, Air Niugini. The word Kumul is also used in PNG to represent national pride, such as in the PNG Kumuls, the country's national rugby league team.

Kina: Official currency in Papua New Guinea which is abbreviated to the currency code PGK (Papua New Guinea Kina). 1K=100 toea. There are coins for toeas and coins for 1K. The rest are banknotes. It was introduced in 1975 when PNG gained independence from Australia and replaced the Australian dollar (AUD).

The name "Kina" comes from a traditional shell money used in PNG's highlands before colonial times.

The Kina's value fluctuates and is affected by PNG's major industries like gold, copper, agriculture (coffee, palm oil, cocoa), and natural gas exports.

Meri Blouse: It's a loose, flowy and brightly coloured blouse, with floral or patterned fabric that woman in PNG wear for everyday comfort. It is valued for its modesty and it is part of their cultural identity. It has been used since missionaries arrived in PNG in the 19th and early 20th centuries, aiming to spread Christianity and Western custom.

Mumu: It is a traditional earth oven used in PNG to cook food. It involves heating stones in a pit, wrapping food (like meat, vegetables, and sweet potatoes) in banana leaves, and then covering it with earth to slow-cook for several hours. A mumu feast is often prepared for special occasions, celebrations, and gatherings. It's an important part of PNG culture.

PMV: It is what public buses are called in PNG. It stands for Public Motor Vehicle. Although it is not a Tok Pisin word, it is the term commonly used for a bus.

Tok Pisin also called "Pidgin", is one of the official languages of PNG and the most widely spoken in the country. It is an English-based creole language with influences from German, Portuguese and many local languages. It is spoken in daily life, politics, business and media. While English is used for formal education and government, Tok Pisin is often the language that unites people from different languages backgrounds.

Wantok: Literally translated to "One Talk" or "One language". It refers to a strong social and kinship system based on shared language, culture or regional ties. Wantoks support each other financially, socially and in daily life, sometimes even over formal institutions. The wantok system is both a source of solidarity and a challenge since it fosters community support but can also lead to favouritism in business and politics.

APPENDIX

A little bit of history about New Guinea Island

To understand how, now-a-days, the island of New Guinea includes two countries we must first reflect on the history of its Indigenous peoples, early contact with Europe and colonisation.

Indigenous people are the people that lived and existed in a land from the earliest times (from before the time that explorers and colonists arrived). It is believed that these people originally travelled from Africa around 50000-70000 years ago via South-East Asia.

Colonisation is the process of people from another place settling among and establishing control over the Indigenous people of a place.

The whole island of New Guinea was divided into two parts in the late 19th century, during the colonial era, mainly due to European colonisation: the Netherlands (Holland) and Germany, later joined by Britain (and eventually Australia). The division became permanent in the 20th century as Indonesia and PNG took their modern form as separate countries living in one big island.

What happened in West Papua?

From the 16th century, Tidore Island, a small kingdom in what is now Indonesia, had trade and friendly relationships with the western part of New Guinea (today's West Papua). They traded spices and sometimes exchanged gifts to maintain their friendship.

In the 17th century, the Netherlands began taking control of many Indonesian islands. They created a large colony called the Dutch East Indies, which corresponds to modern-day Indonesia. Later, the Dutch used their historical connection with Tidore to claim West Papua.

In 1828, the Netherlands officially took control of the western half of New Guinea and called it Dutch New Guinea. They mostly ruled the coastal areas and worked with local leaders to manage villages.

During World War II (1939–1945), Japan invaded and controlled parts of West Papua. They stayed for a few years until Australia and the United States helped defeat them.

After the war, the Dutch returned and tried to prepare West Papua for independence, but Indonesia, which became independent in 1949, wanted West Papua to join the country.

In 1962, the United Nations helped to make a deal: the Dutch left, and the territory was temporarily administered by the UN. In 1963, West Papua officially became part of Indonesia.

In 1969, Indonesia held a vote (called the "Act of Free Choice") to decide if West Papua would stay with Indonesia. Only a small group of local leaders voted, and they all said yes, but many Papuans felt the vote was unfair.

Today, some people in West Papua still hope for independence or greater rights. Many identify themselves as Papuan rather than Indonesian, which has led to ongoing political tensions.

What happened in East Papua?

The eastern half of Papua was divided in 1884 between Germany (North-East New Guinea/German New Guinea) and Britain (South-East New Guinea/British New Guinea).

In 1906 Britain transferred its Papuan territory to Australia.

During World War I, in 1914, Australia invaded the German New Guinea colony and assumed control of the entire Eastern half of the island.

In World War II, the Japanese mostly invaded the northern and coastal parts of the eastern half of Papua and their troops advanced within 50kms of capturing Port Moresby. PNG and Australian soldiers, trackers and tribesman made significant contributions during this war. Many lives were lost 250,000 people were killed or wounded across PNG. To this day, Australia and PNG share a close bond over what happened in PNG during World War II. The Kokoda Track is famous for remembering this. The impact of war on PNG and its people was massive, and it became inevitable that the country would demand political equality and even independence.

Once World War II ended in 1945, under a United Nations Trusteeship Agreement, Australia took control of both territories and in 1949, they officially became Papua New Guinea. So, for 30 years there was pressure for independence, but political change was very slow. After years of PNG leaders pushing for independence, it finally came on the 16th of September 1975 without bloodshed.

Papua New Guineans, generally, do not feel hostile towards Australia, they view that when Australia was in administration, they supported PNG leaders towards self-government and they are thankful. PNG is incredibly proud and happy to celebrate their independence!

Today, the indigenous peoples of Papua New Guinea identify as Papuan or Melanesian. It is very important to respect that amongst the Indigenous peoples of PNG there are hundreds of different groups known as clans (or language groups) and most will have their own explanations about the universe, each with differing beliefs and practices.

Not all PNG people are the same! With over 800 clans and languages this country is one of the most linguistically and culturally diverse places in the world.

Travelling Twins Next Adventure

After six years of living in Papua New Guinea, our South Pacific Ocean adventure came to an end. Closing one chapter and turning the page to another phase of live can be exciting for some and difficult for others, or both at the same time, but either way, life continues. Thankfully it does.

We are about to embrace another culture, another religion, another gastronomy that includes insects, apparently the primary source of protein for next generations and another way of living in South East Asia. Cambodia is our next stop and we can't wait to share our experience with you.

ACKNOWLEDGEMENTS

Thank you to Andy, my husband and the father of our girls, Clàudia and Júlia.

Our life together has been full of adventures and numerous challenges.

What makes him so special is that he believes and supports all my projects.

That's the reason why you can have this book in your hands.

Thank you to my parents, Josep and Magda, for their unconditional love. They have given support to me and my sisters, Magda and Ester, embracing our different personalities and decisions beyond comparison.

Thank you to my mother-in-law, Beryl, and my step-children, Kaitlin and Jett, for their countless grammar edits.

Thank you to my PNG girlfriends who took their time to read the book and made suggestions that I took on board. Thanks to Megan Toka, Jade Aiton, Alana Uechtritz, Luisa Cakaukeivuya, Madonna Stow, Margaret O'Sullivan, Dorothy Kenneth, and, last but not least, Sandy Edwards for your precious time invested on making this book more accurate.

A special thank you to all the PNG people who gave me permission to use their real life experiences in this book. You all know who you are. Your names have been changed to protect your privacy.

Thank you also to the mums who allowed me to use their daughter's real name.

Thanks to Carolina Evari, a local author who collaborated with me at the start of my PNG writing adventure. I found in her the encouragement to develop my idea and pursue my dream.

Thank you to all my friends in Spain that have always believed I could become an author and repeatedly encouraged me to write.

About The Author

 Núria was born in 1974 in Catalonia, Spain and fulfilled her dream to become a high school teacher, a mentor and a principal of a public school.

Although she travelled a lot around the world during her holidays she never lived abroad until her late 30s.

A personal crisis prompted her to travel to Australia and start a new life on the other side of the world following her dream of improving her English and working in another Education System.

There, she met her husband and together created a blended family and new adventures in Papua New Guinea where she kept working as a teacher and started writing this book.

Currently she lives in Cambodia and can keep teaching. She has learnt to prioritise what makes her happy, so she has kept swimming, learning languages, writing and enjoying her family and friends' time.

Living in different countries has opened her mind to other ways of living, other ways of parenting, other religions, etc. A humbling experience that gave her a greater appreciation of her own culture and renewed respect for different ways of living.

She has written two family books about her origin and ancestors, she is writing an extensive journal of her twin daughter's lives but this is her first published book, a big achievement. I hope you enjoy it.

2026 – first print published by Ultimate World Publishing

ISBN

Paperback: 978-1-923425-27-9
Ebook: 978-1-923425-28-6

Written & created by Núria Cort Lluís

Cover design: Ultimate World Publishing

Layout and typesetting: Ultimate World Publishing

Editor: Vanessa MacKay

Illustrations: Ultimate World Publishing

Ultimate World Publishing
Diamond Creek,
Victoria Australia 3089
www.writeabook.com.au